American Roots

CALVIN SHORTS

A series published by the Calvin College Press

American Roots

by James D. Bratt

COLLEGE
Grand Rapids, MI · calvin.edu/press

Published 2016 by the Calvin College Press
3201 Burton St. SE
Grand Rapids, MI 49546

Publisher's Cataloging-in-Publication data
Names: Bratt, James D., 1949-, author.
Title: American roots / James D. Bratt.
Series: Calvin Shorts.
Description: Grand Rapids, MI: Calvin College Press, 2016.
Identifiers: ISBN 978-1-937555-19-1 (pbk.) | ISBN 978-1-937555-20-7 (ebook) | LCCN 2016936744
Subjects: LCSH United States--History--1600-1775, Colonial period. | United States--History--Colonial period, ca. 1600-1775. | Great Britain--Colonies--America--History--16th century. | America--Colonization. | United States--Politics and government--To 1775. | BISAC HISTORY / United States / Colonial Period (1600-1775) | HISTORY / African American | HISTORY / United States / State & Local / New England (CT, MA, ME, NH, RI, VT) | HISTORY / United States / State & Local / Middle Atlantic (DC, DE, MD, NJ, NY, PA) | HISTORY / United States / State & Local / South (AL, AR, FL, GA, KY, LA, MS, NC, SC, TN, VA, Classification: LCC E188 .B785 2016 | DDC 973.2—dc23

Cover design: Robert Alderink

Maps created by Peter Bratt, from originals in David Hackett Fischer, *Albion's Seed: Four British Folkways in America* (New York and Oxford: Oxford University Press, 1989), and Alan Taylor, *American Colonies: The Settling of North America* (New York: Penguin, 2001).

Contents

*To all the students in my Early America course
at Calvin College, 1987–2014*

Series Editor's Foreword

Midway along the journey of our life
I woke to find myself in some dark woods,
For I had wandered off from the straight path.

So begins *The Divine Comedy*, a classic meditation on the Christian life, written by Dante Alighieri in the fourteenth century.

Dante's three images—a journey, a dark forest, and a perplexed pilgrim—still feel familiar today, don't they?

We can readily imagine our own lives as a series of journeys, not just the big journey from birth to death, but also all the little trips from home to school, from school to job, from place to place, from old friends to new. In fact, we often feel we are simultaneously on multiple journeys that tug us in diverse and sometimes opposing directions. We recognize those dark woods from fairy tales and nightmares and the all-too-real conundrums that crowd our everyday lives. No wonder we frequently feel perplexed. We wake up shaking our heads, unsure if we know how to live wisely today or tomorrow or next week.

This series has in mind just such perplexed pilgrims. Each book invites you, the reader, to walk alongside experienced guides who will help you understand the contours of the road as well as the surrounding landscape. They will cut back the underbrush, untangle myths and misconceptions, and suggest ways to move forward.

And they will do it in books intended to be read in an evening or during a flight. Calvin Shorts are designed not just for perplexed pilgrims, but also for busy ones. We live in a complex and changing world. We need nimble ways to acquire knowledge, skills, and wisdom. These books are one way to meet those needs.

John Calvin, after whom this series is named, recognized our pilgrim condition. "We are always on the road," he said, and although this road, this life, is full of perplexities, it is also "a gift of divine kindness which is not to be refused." Calvin Shorts takes as its starting point this claim that we are called to live well in a world that is both gift and challenge.

In *The Divine Comedy*, Dante's guide is Virgil, a wise but not omniscient mentor. So too, the authors in the Calvin Shorts series don't pretend to know it all. They, like you and me, are pilgrims. And they invite us to walk with them as together we seek to live more faithfully in this world that belongs to God.

Susan M. Felch
Executive Editor
The Calvin College Press

Additional Resources

Additional online resources for *American Roots* may be available at http://www.calvin.edu/press.

Introduction

HISTORY AS STORY

Every history contains a story. This is true in the literal spelling of the word but also on a deeper, more important level. In writing history, we choose a relatively few data from the nearly infinite supply out there in the past. We use these data to give an account of what happened back then and how that helps us make better sense of our lives today. To change the image, we select particular beads out of a big tub and put them on a string for people to appreciate and try on. The beads draw the eye, but the string is what keeps them together. Likewise, a story-line gives unity and thrust to the various facts of history. It helps us answer: what do these facts add up to? What is our history all about?

This book tries to answer these questions for early America. Most Americans remember the colonial period in bits and pieces from a high school history class. Often the pieces are connected to particular stories. There's Pocahontas rescuing Captain John Smith from execution at the hands of her father. There are the Pilgrims hosting the first Thanksgiving feast at Plymouth Rock. There's the Salem witch craze, the battle of Bunker Hill, the Constitutional Convention, and so on. A couple of problems immediately arise out of these stories. Take the one about

Pocahontas for instance. Her father, the paramount chief of the native Powhatan Confederacy, probably did not want to execute John Smith but claim him as a subject or at least an ally for political purposes. Maybe the fake-death and redemption ritual was meant to seal that deal. Or maybe the event did not happen at all. Smith sometimes talked about the episode but sometimes ignored it, making it hard to decide this question for sure. Part of the historian's challenge, then, is to determine which stories are authentic. The other part, and the one we are concerned with right here, is to determine how the data that have been authenticated come together. What is the keyword we should use to string all the particular bits and pieces together to make a narrative that is true and relevant and helpful? More briefly, what's the main theme of early American history?

TWO STORY-LINES

Many Americans would probably answer that question with "America" itself. In this telling, the story of the colonial period is the story of thousands of Europeans crossing the Atlantic Ocean in search of a new way of life. Soon they came to feel that their new land needed political independence, too. They begin and win the American Revolution. End of story, beginning of a new nation. But there are problems with this account. First, there were many non-Europeans on the scene, of whom more in a minute. Second, many of those Europeans were not interested in a new way of life. Instead, they wanted a new chance at an old, familiar life that had become impossible back home. Third, in thinking about their new land, they did not have in mind the whole stretch of thirteen colonies that we are familiar with from maps in school. They thought of the particular colony in which they lived, or just the part of the colony that they were familiar with: this stretch of the Hudson River, a cluster of towns in backcountry Massachusetts. Since it might well have been easier to get from their nearest seaport to England than to another port along the American coast, they more likely had a "British" as well as a local identity than an "American" one. In fact, "American," used as a term for people rather than the name of a territory, only came into use after 1740. It was first uttered by British officers in response to the provincials on this shore who greeted them as fellow "Englishmen." "You aren't English; you're American," they sneered. Even then, it took the colonists a long time to think about changing their political allegiance. Not until 1770 at the earliest, or even after the battle of Lexington and Concord (1775) had shed American blood, did many of them begin to think in terms of political independence.

Another keyword for our story might be "liberty," or perhaps a couplet, "liberty" and "equality." But here again we run into problems. By the time the new United States was founded in 1776, fully twenty percent of its inhabitants shared in neither liberty nor equality. They were enslaved, and this slavery was not a fluke or a bad old habit on the way out. It was essential to the fabric of the new nation. The number of slaves and their importance to the economy had steadily increased from 1675 to 1775. If white settlers and their descendants felt that America was indeed a land of liberty—and many did, with good cause—the economy built on slavery was in no small part responsible for that freedom. At the same time, more and more white people felt they were falling short of equality too, even if they were free. If slavery had grown over the last century, so too had land tenancy. On the eve of Independence, more wealth was under the command of fewer people than ever before. True, the situation was better than in most of Europe, but our subjects did not live in Europe. They lived in New Jersey or Connecticut or Virginia. There they saw property-less men flocking to the cities, looking for jobs. Or working on land that they could never hope to own. Or stopped from getting married by the lack of economic prospects.

The golden age of equality turned out to have come at the very start of the colonial period, when everybody was more or less in the same plain boat. We usually take the story of liberty and equality to mean that the passage of time brings "progress." That is, time is supposed to be a tide that will lift most boats. As it turned out, "progress" in colonial America had lifted some boats much more than others. Yet another idea tied to the theme of liberty and equality is "freedom of religion." But freedom of religion figured in the founding of only a few of the thirteen colonies. And only two of them, Rhode Island and Pennsylvania, regarded the term the same way as we do—freedom to worship as you please. In the rest of New England it meant freedom to worship God not as you pleased but as God pleased. Ministers, supported by the tax dollars of all the citizens, were there to tell you exactly how.

AND YET ONE MORE

If these familiar story-lines are not true—or are only partly so—then what story should we tell ourselves about our American roots instead?

Perhaps we should return to the original motto of the United States: *e pluribus unum*; "out of many, one." By "many" the Founders probably had in mind the thirteen states that were being joined into one nation. But for understanding the roots of the United States, it makes more sense to talk not about thirteen states but about five regions. Each of these regions was defined by a particular geography, and each attracted a particular set of people from across the Atlantic. These immigrants brought with them their own stories, their own pictures of a proper society, along with a particular set of governing values and religious loyalties. They established different kinds of economies. Although they had much in common, and although time brought the regions closer together on some counts, the differences remained—and sometimes even grew stronger. The *unum* of the new nation was more of a goal than a reality.

And so it remains today. One purpose of this book is to push past nostalgia for a golden age of peace and harmony that never was. The United States from the start has been an argument, although ideally it has been an argument conducted without violence within the bounds of the Constitution. Some of our current quarrels started only recently, but others go back to differences established already in colonial times. This book hopes to show where, why, and with what consequences those differences emerged so that we can better understand early Americans—and ourselves today.

FIVE REGIONS, THREE RACES

Because colonial America can be understood as five distinct regions, we will look at each of these in turn. We will visit each region asking the same sorts of questions that anthropologists ask when they travel to a new country: What are the hopes, values, and ideas that different people brought along with them when they arrived in the Americas? How did their new environment change them? What other changes came with time? What persisted from their old life? Many newcomers may have hoped less for a new way of life than a new chance at an old one. Yet time, place, and chance happened to them all so that a new sort of life *did* emerge in British North America. At the same time, the different hopes, dreams, and values of their original plans still showed through.

And there was more. In their new environment, European colonists encountered not just a new landscape but also native peoples they had not previously known. This native population would soon fall in numbers due to foreign diseases, harsh treatment, and eviction from their lands, but Indians still outnumbered Euro-Americans east of the Mississippi River well into the eighteenth century. Then their territory came into the cross-hairs of rival European empires. In the resulting wars, the native peoples were of key strategic importance. Local leaders knew this when they advised British General Edward Braddock to cultivate Indian allies, at least as scouts, in invading western Pennsylvania in 1755. Braddock ignored them. He paid with his life when a French and Indian force surprised and slaughtered his army short of its target of Fort Duquesne. The native peoples had a cultural influence, too. When young Bostonians disguised themselves as Mohawk warriors to conduct the "tea party" in 1773, they showed how deeply the Indian presence had sifted into white Americans' identity. To be a Mohawk was to be an American. Yet because most Indians lived outside of white settlements, they were still considered outsiders. For most of early American history and beyond, Indian concerns seemed more like "foreign policy" than "internal affairs."

It was just the opposite with the other major race

that appeared on the scene, people from Africa. Within a century of contact with Europeans, nearly eighty percent of the native Indian population died off. Africans were forced into the breach. From 1492 until 1815, an equal eighty percent of all people who crossed the Atlantic were Africans bound in chains. They became deeply integrated into the white-run economies, even as they were thoroughly subordinated in white society. They suffered horrendous mortality rates, principally because the vast majority of them were bound to grueling plantation labor under the tropical sun in Brazil and the Caribbean, and secondly because the enslavers' strong preference for males over females limited the birth rate.

In the eighteenth century, the only exception to these high mortality rates occurred among the Africans enslaved in the southern regions and northern seaports of what would become the United States. By mid-century, they constituted a majority in South Carolina, the majority of the work force in Virginia, and twenty percent of the population of New York City. Although these future Americans represented only five percent of all the people brought over from Africa, by 1950 they proved to be the ancestors of one-third of all people of African descent in the Western Hemisphere. In sum, while Indians were kept to the fringe, Africans entered into the center of white life in three of colonial America's five regions. Black and white life were shaped accordingly.

OUR TRAVEL PLANNER

And so we begin our tour of colonial America's five regions. We start with the oldest persisting British settlement in the New World, the Chesapeake region of Virginia and Maryland, begun at Jamestown in 1607. We then move down to the Lower South of the Carolinas and Georgia, which looked toward the intensive slave-labor sugar colony of Barbados. Carolina's founders were sons of Barbadian elites who carried the island's model over to the mainland. We then move up to New England, where the tale of colonial American history has traditionally begun. We don't begin in New England because, being religiously driven and the first free-labor set of settlements, New England was the exception to the slave-labor rule for colonizing the Western Hemisphere. The fourth region, the Middle Colonies of New York, New Jersey, and Pennsylvania, was also mostly built on free labor. Unlike New England, however, the Middle Colonies attracted a motley array of European immigrants. This region came to be defined above all by ethnic and religious diversity as well as high levels of trade through their large ports of New York and Philadelphia. Through those ports flowed an increasingly large tide of immigrants from Scotland and the north of Ireland over the course of the eighteenth century. These newcomers settled in the colonial backcountry which became the fifth distinctive, and perhaps most turbulent, region of colonial America.

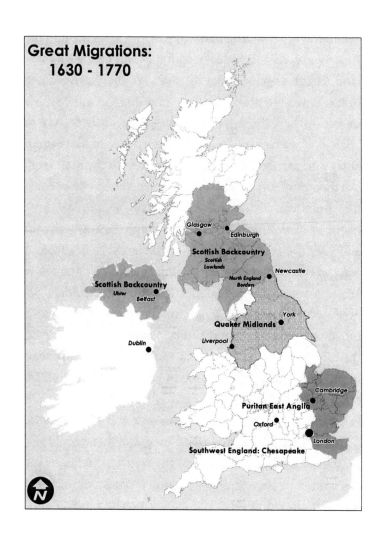

Great Migrations:
1630 - 1770

Glasgow
Edinburgh

Scottish Backcountry
Scottish Lowlands

North England Borders
Newcastle

Scottish Backcountry
Ulster
Belfast

York

Quaker Midlands
Liverpool

Dublin

Cambridge

Puritan East Anglia
Oxford

London

Southwest England: Chesapeake

N

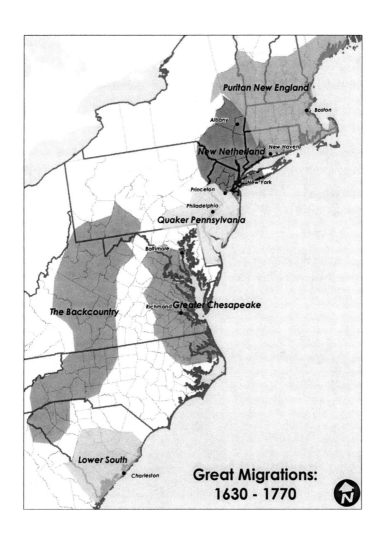

Puritan New England

Boston

Albany

New Netherland

New Haven

New York

Princeton

Philadelphia

Quaker Pennsylvania

Baltimore

The Backcountry

Richmond Greater Chesapeake

Lower South

Charleston

Great Migrations:
1630 - 1770

The chapters that follow analyze each region, one by one. For each we will first survey the land and the people who settled there and how they were shaped by its particular geography. Second, we'll look at a defining crisis in its history, an episode that reveals in sharp relief the dominant values of its system and the contradictions it harbored. Third, we'll note some of the leading legacies that each region gave to the independent nation. It was the mix of these varied ingredients, however unlikely the odds, that went into the building of the new nation. This nation would have a raucous infancy, a near-fatal adolescence, and an adulthood that still bears the marks and spirit of its origins. Americans continue to draw off these roots. Non-Americans can look at these roots to understand the massive tree that still looms large, for better or worse, on the world scene today.

The
Chesapeake

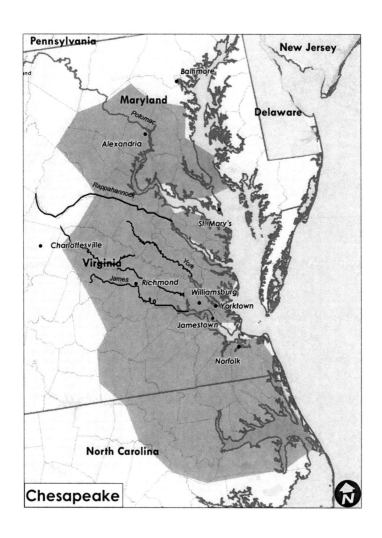

Pennsylvania

New Jersey

Baltimore

Maryland

Delaware

Potomac

Alexandria

Rappahannock

St. Mary's

Charlottesville

Virginia

York

James   Richmond

Williamsburg

Yorktown

Jamestown

Norfolk

North Carolina

Chesapeake

The great tidal rivers off Chesapeake Bay—the James, York, Rappahannock, and Potomac—fundamentally shaped the English settlements that grew there, starting with Jamestown in 1607. The estates along those rivers could load ocean-going goods at their front door. This was not only convenient for the owners of these estates, but also gave them control of their neighbors' trade. Over time these estates expanded and included their own craftsmen—blacksmiths, carpenters, and the like. Maps of colonial Virginia show very few towns; there was no need to "go to town" to buy your goods. Instead, "courthouses" at crossroads defined the landscape and the culture. Virginians got together through the languages and contests of law.

But building up big estates with a profitable product took a long time. The men who established Jamestown— and males held a 6:1 majority—were "adventurers." They undertook high risks for big rewards. They had in mind the treasures of gold and silver that the Spanish had found in Mexico and Peru. When the banks of the James River disappointed on that score, they tried other schemes instead, planting vineyards or mulberry trees for silk- worms. What they did not plant was food. They waited to be resupplied by ships from their corporate sponsor, or they raided Indian stores, inciting lethal attacks in return, or they starved. They died in droves—ninety percent of them in the first fifteen years—and by 1624 their sponsor, the Virginia Company, went bankrupt. The king took it over; investors back home had land titles but no profits.

Yet economic salvation had already appeared. Tobacco plants imported from Spanish holdings in South America seeded a profitable cash crop. Virginia's gold proved to be brown. Smoking and snuff turned into such a craze in London that King James tried, in vain, to ban it. But cultivating tobacco—planting, weeding, picking, curing, and packing it—turned out to require a lot of labor. The planters found that they could not force the local Indians to work in the way the conquistadors had managed in Mexico, so they turned to another source instead. England, as it happened, had developed a large surplus population due to rising fertility rates and falling demand for farm labor. More and more land was being turned into pastures for wool production, and tending sheep required less work than tilling the soil. The displaced workers flocked to the cities, especially to London, the prototype of the urban slum-sprawl we see around the world today. London was literally a toxic environment, but still the footloose young men poured in. Alternatively, they wandered in gangs around the countryside. When they ran afoul of the law, when they woke up from a drunken spree, when they decided that the bad odds of survival in the New World were still better than those in the grim city, they set off for Virginia. The cost of their passage was paid by planters on their arrival, in exchange for a set length (four to seven years, typically) of indentured service. While retaining more rights than slaves would in years to come, these were bondsmen, and their masters were determined to extract full value from their labor.

Only a minority survived their term to reap their reward—fifty acres of land and tools to start a farm of their own. Many problems still stood in their way. They had to establish legal title to their claim, which required surveyor and courtroom skills. Then they had to survive the year needed to clear the land, plant, and take the first harvest. Soon the best river-front acres were gone, and the temptation to poach on Indian territory increased, with predictable results. All in all, early Virginia resembled a mining camp—competitive, violent, crassly materialistic, and full of single, rootless young men determined to get rich quick. But as more of them survived, Virginia started to resemble the old country as well—fewer landowners, more tenant farmers. Now disgruntled young men roamed about the Virginia countryside, armed and dangerous.

Another problem from the old world soon moved to the new. As civil war wracked England across the 1640s, some of the affluent shareholders in the old Virginia Company sent sons to the New World. Why not get them out of harm's way at home by taking over that land patent which had been lying idle in the desk drawer? These sons arrived on the scene with social as well as financial capital: higher education, familiarity with law, family connections.

They fared well, acquiring more land, more servants, and some ex-servants as tenants. These were the founders of the great First Families that would come to dominate the colony in the years ahead: the Carters, Byrds, Harrisons, Randolphs, and Lees.

But all was not well. In 1660, though peace had returned to England, ominous pressures kept building in Virginia. Tobacco prices plunged due to over-supply. The price of land—good land—rose because of short supply. England's population surplus had tapered off too, so fewer new indentured servants arrived. Men who had survived their terms looked, in vain, for the reward for their enormous risk. Some of the new elite were angry as well. William Berkeley, the royal governor, turned Virginia into a textbook case of crony capitalism. Planters with inside connections got plum posts as county officials, tobacco assessors, or even a seat on the governor's council. They held a monopoly on the lucrative Indian trade, supposedly arranged to keep peace on the frontier. They had an inside track on promising land deals. Some of the new rich men had a hard time breaking into this charmed circle. The already noticeable class divide widened.

THE DEFINING CRISIS

All of these forces converged in Virginia's defining crisis, Bacon's Rebellion of 1676. Nathaniel Bacon was a classic elite newcomer—a Cambridge graduate and Governor

Berkeley's relative. He wanted frontier land, and using a skirmish with Doeg Indians as a pretext, he demanded that Berkeley commission him to lead a raid against the Indians. When Berkeley refused, Bacon marched his men off anyway and fell upon another tribe that had no part in the original incident. Soon the whole frontier was aflame. Berkeley responded with an expensive proposal to erect a string of forts to keep the peace. But Bacon and his angry young men didn't want peace; they wanted land. They turned around and marched on the capital, forcing Berkeley to flee across the James River. Bacon in turn took refuge in the swamps, where he promptly died. His rebellion fell apart.

Yet the uprising had its effect. The Crown was so upset by the disruption of the tobacco trade—by now one of its key sources of revenue—that it instituted some dramatic reforms. Berkeley was fired, insider privilege was reduced, and terms of the tobacco trade were better regulated. But these were not moves toward democracy. Rather, the reforms merely stabilized Virginia's hierarchy by allowing the new elite men to join the older ones at the top. The hierarchy was also stabilized, fatefully, by a new floor—enslaved Africans who would have no chance to become free and who would provide a firm and stable foundation for those who were already rich or aimed to become so.

From 1619 on, Africans had been in the cargos of the young men who came to the Chesapeake, but they had not all been enslaved from the start. Some held regular indentures, and a few survived to become landowners and masters themselves. That ambiguity ended in the 1660s when the Virginia legislature passed a series of racially based laws. All African imports, and only they, would henceforth be treated as enslaved for life, and that status would pass down to any children they might have. Still, with only six percent of the population being of African descent, Virginia remained in 1670 a society with slaves rather than a slave society. But then came Bacon's Rebellion. At the same time, the Royal African Company was chartered back in London to boost trade with that continent. At once England's mainland colonies had a more reliable supply of and a much greater demand for slave labor. The African percentage of Virginia's population rose steadily, to forty-four percent by 1750.

LASTING LEGACIES

This rise was particularly striking given the sharp increase in the colony's population as a whole. Around 1680, the white gender ratio had finally evened out enough to produce a natural increase in the population. After seventy-five years, Virginia was no longer an immigrant society. By 1740, it was Britain's largest mainland colony in population as well as territory. Political and social stability improved off these trends, aided by some crucial cultural reinforcement. Virginians observed a set of practices, rituals, and values that translated mere power into recognized authority. The contours of that authority fit with Virginia's old-world roots. Its original settlers tended to come from the southern counties of England where society was presumed to be a hierarchy in which the "better people" ruled and "lesser" folk obeyed. Establishing who was "better" and "lesser" in this wilderness had involved no little tumult, featuring raw force, bald assertion, and sheer luck. The men who rose to the top of the heap needed to show that they deserved to stay there. They did so by demonstrating their mastery of fortune and of other people.

If we had visited Virginia around 1750, we could have seen this process at work at four different sites, beginning in the fields. The first sign of mastery was to return a prized tobacco crop year after year. It required sound judgment to know exactly the right time to plant and harvest, and the best way to cure and pack. It also required the master to command some of the "fear" that the Bible associates with God. Planters tried to keep the enslaved at work with a minimum of force, although they could be remorseless if needed. The second site was church. Everyone was expected to attend church, but if you were part of the elite group, you entered the service only after the minister had begun. That showed everyone who was really in charge. Third, just as the courthouse defined the Chesapeake's map, the courtroom was the crucial site for proving status. It was vital to maintain one's land claims against rivals, and since planters functioned as their own lawyers, knowledge of law and the ability to persuade were highly prized skills.

The jury's verdict announced exactly where you stood. So did the process of public voting if you were bold enough to stand for office. This fourth drama, of polling day, might coincide with the militia muster, where you could demonstrate your ability to command men in battle. And when all such business was completed, the entertainments of the day continued the lesson. Horse racing showed one's mastery of animals; high-stakes wagering put your money where your mouth was; and dancing late into the night let the ladies vote who they thought was the better man.

And so Virginia became the hierarchical society that traditionalists in the old world took to be natural. Forty percent of its inhabitants provided the base of enslaved labor. Twenty percent were landless tenants; twenty-five percent more were yeomen of some property. For the yeomen and for a smaller number of gentry above them, the promise of "liberty"—economic autonomy—had come true. At the top of the pyramid the dream turned out sweeter still. From here came an outsized share of the political and military leadership that went into the making of the American nation: George Washington, commander of the army; Thomas Jefferson, prime author of the Declaration of Independence; James Madison, of the Constitution; and John Marshall, key chief justice of the Supreme Court. Virginia supplied four of the nation's first six presidents and a line of military commanders that stretched from Washington through the twentieth century: Robert E. Lee and Thomas ("Stonewall") Jackson; George Patton and

George Marshall, graduates of the Virginia Military Institute; and William Westmoreland of Vietnam infamy, who bore the name of an original Virginia county. The national capital was carved out of Maryland territory. Across the Potomac in Virginia today loom the symbols of the military establishment: the Pentagon and the headquarters of the CIA.

3

The Lower
South

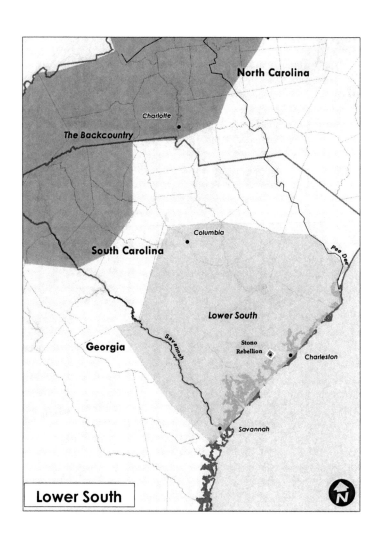

North Carolina

Charlotte

The Backcountry

South Carolina

Columbia

Pee Dee

Lower South

Savannah

Stono Rebellion

Charleston

Georgia

Savannah

Lower South

While the Chesapeake evolved toward slavery, the colonies of the Lower South pursued it from the start. They had learned from the masters of the craft, the planters of Barbados. By 1650, that tiny island was England's richest and most populous New World colony.

Barbados had begun, in the 1620s, as a copy of Virginia, but soon adopted the formula that turned it and the other islands of the Caribbean into the crown jewels of their respective empires. This was the sugar plantation worked under the tropical sun by African slave labor. Europe seemed ready to buy rum, molasses, and refined sugar without limit. Financial and human capital poured into the lands that could produce those goods. The Portuguese had carried this model from the Mediterranean to the West African coast and then to their colony in Brazil. One third of the vast African tide to the Western Hemisphere went there. Another half went to the Caribbean. Between Brazil and the Caribbean, the slave-labor plantation set the standard for New World colonization. It rewarded a small white elite with enormous wealth, but also put them on top of an explosive pyramid populated by a vast enslaved majority. It required enormous capital as well. On an island like Barbados, middling planters, not to mention the poor whites who had survived indentured servitude, were soon driven out. They and the surplus sons of the elite looked first to Jamaica (acquired by England in 1655) for their own chance at the game. Others turned toward the mainland colony that had been chartered in 1663 in the name of King Charles II.

Carolina would be divided into North and South in 1712, but the southern half and its capital of Charleston would remain the center of Lower South development through the Revolution. Its climate didn't suit sugar cane, so the planters' sons at first sorted through other possibilities. One of the most lucrative was a slave trade of their own. They set local Indians to war against each other and sold the captives to Caribbean plantations. As those plantations produced little food of their own, the Carolinians began raising beef cattle on their open lands. But who knew how to raise good beef? The slaves who were brought over from the African savannahs, where cattle herding was familiar. The cowboys, round-ups, and corrals ("Cowpens") so familiar in American stories started here. The Western really should be called the "Southern."

Carolinians also launched hunting parties deep into the interior. Eventually 150,000 deerskins a year were being exported out of Charleston and New Orleans. But the long-term staples turned out to be rice, for export abroad, and indigo, valued for its royal purple dye. Again, West African experience with these crops proved vital for success. Enslaved labor built the levees and sluice gates needed for irrigating the fields, and performed the hard work of leveling the fields and planting, cultivating, and harvesting rice in them. Rice wasn't sugar, but the profits were fine enough and the consequences familiar. By 1720 South Carolina had a seventy percent black majority. The ratio was as high as 8:1 in the "Low Country" plantations along the coast. A European traveler who toured the mainland colonies just before the Revolution remarked that Charleston was the only American city that could compare with Paris. He meant it as a compliment. Thomas Jefferson and others would take it as an indictment. Both capitals sat atop a highly productive countryside worked by exploited labor. Carolina featured the additional complication of race.

THE DEFINING CRISIS

Carolina's defining crisis therefore was a slave insurrection, the Stono Rebellion of 1739, named after the district west of Charleston where it arose. Angered by some planters' violation of tacit agreements about the terms of work, some twenty men attacked on Sunday morning, September 9. They targeted the homes of the offensive owners, bypassing others. They killed two dozen whites, gathered another sixty recruits, and headed south. England was newly at war with Spain, and Spanish authorities in Florida promised freedom to any escapees who would join their cause. Some of the Stono leaders were experienced warriors, too, having been trained in the Kongo (Angola) from where Carolina drew most of its labor. A number were also baptized Roman Catholics and may have chosen the celebration of Mary's saint day to stage their uprising. In any case, the Carolina planters panicked. They formed squadrons to hunt down and kill the rebels. They passed a severe new slave code that became a model for the South. It required whites to carry arms and operate night patrols, forbade black assemblies and literacy, and restricted slaves' mobility and manumission. The planters even managed to reduce slave importations for a time, although by the 1750s the numbers starting ticking up again. At the time of the Revolution, South Carolina would be the one state with an enslaved majority. Therein lay its fortune, and fate.

LASTING LEGACIES

To maximize safety and control, South Carolina's political system was the most centralized, homogenous, and elite of all the colonies. Its leaders knew that faction would be fatal and so praised "the harmony for which we are famous"—that is, they quashed dissent. Poorer whites were disenfranchised in the process, lest economic rivalry disrupt rule. The regime also kept all power in Charleston itself. Other colonies planted courts in the backcountry; South Carolina did not. Any plaintiff had to carry his suit to the capital, at great expense. Above all, Carolinians feared "outsiders" intervening in their affairs. These outsiders might be ambitious Virginians, against whom they would stir up Indian assaults. They might be British officials, against whom they took the risky step of revolution. After Independence the list of outsiders would include federal tariff legislation, which South Carolina pretended to "nullify" under a theory propounded by its senator, John C. Calhoun; abolitionists, whose pamphlets they barred from the mails; and a Republican presidency, against which they fired on at Fort Sumter and so began the Civil War. A century later amid the civil rights movement, the villain became "outside agitators" alleged to have riled up "our contented Negroes." The "Dixie-crat" exodus from the Democratic Party convention in 1948, led by South Carolina Senator Strom Thurmond, marked the beginning of the white shift to the Republican column that has made the old Confederacy the hard core of that party. Thurmond was simply following in the line of Calhoun and of the Barbadians before him.

South Carolina exerted a magnetic pull on the two other colonies of the Lower South, even though they began with different priorities. North Carolina at first attracted ordinary whites fleeing the turn toward slavery in Virginia and South Carolina. It also was the one place in the South of interest to the mass of German immigrants who started to cross the Atlantic in the 1720s. But the plantation model eventually overpowered that of the family farm. By Independence, North Carolina had a 2:1 white-black ratio and an investment in maintaining slavery. Even more tragic was the evolution of Georgia. It was established in 1732, first as a defensive barrier against the

Spanish Empire, and second as a place where debtors and other hard-pressed folk from Britain could get a second chance. Georgia was the only colony founded with a ban on slavery, and on rum as well. But the protests from Carolina sons with capital who moved south proved to be too much. In 1752, Georgia lifted its bans on slavery and rum, and it became a clone of its parent to the north.

Slavery was not exactly the same in the various American colonies, however. The patterns of life and labor in the Chesapeake differed significantly from those in the Lower South. In the former, with its white majority, the enslaved typically lived in direct contact with their master. He commanded their labor for the entire day and supervised them closely. He also watched over their conduct after sundown. Consequently, the enslaved in the Chesapeake transitioned earlier to using English. Their labor could be quite varied, involving the many different tasks of tobacco production, plus craft jobs on the larger plantations. They also saw a natural increase in their numbers by the 1730s, a first in the Western Hemisphere, and this despite their lower chances of finding a mate on the same plantation as themselves. They conducted "abroad" relationships on neighboring farms. Nothing so triggered their resistance as when a master interfered with visits to their partners and children. Some of these relationships crossed the racial divide as well, less often with whites than with native peoples in the area.

The Lower South, especially in the Low Country, was

different on most of these counts. There, the enslaved had a much greater chance of living totally amongst themselves, with a slave overseer standing in for an absent master. They worked by a "task" regime, assigned to finish a particular job with the rest of the day for themselves. They devoted that time to cultivating their own small plots where they raised much of the fresh food consumed in Charleston. The markets there were operated by black women. Otherwise, rice production involved less varied labor than tobacco and so taught a narrower skillset than was true of the Chesapeake. Interracial contact with the native population was lower, and more hostile, since planters from the start used blacks in their attacks on Indians, while compensating the latter for returning escaped slaves. Natural increase came to the Lower South slave quarters around the 1750s, and it was more likely to occur via relationships on the same plantation, given the greater number of possible partners there. Meanwhile, since the slave trade boomed here until it was officially closed in 1808, African culture continued to be refreshed in the Lower South, with particular impact on religion and language.

We have said little about religion so far, and this is surprising since the South today is the most churched region in the country. That was not true, however, until after the Civil War, and the process began only late in the colonial era. It took the birth of evangelical Protestantism, the "Great Awakening," to bring organized Christianity to the dispersed population of the rural South. Until then the Church of England had the largest presence, but it lacked the resources to keep up with a booming, mobile population. It stayed mostly at the upper levels of older settlements. It tried to keep order, elevate the moral tone, lessen the scramble for wealth, punish gross abuses, and remind one and all that they lived under transcendent norms of moral accountability. But heaven was high, and the bishops needed to put teeth into this system lived far away. Local churches, like everything else, lived under the dominance of the biggest planters in the neighborhood. In brief, before the Revolution the Chesapeake and Lower South were more societies with churches than churched societies.

4

New England

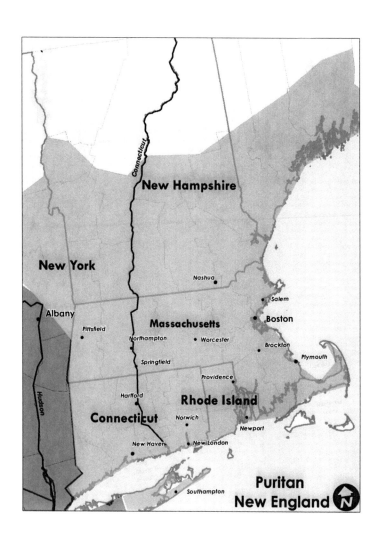

Connecticut

New Hampshire

New York

Nashua

Albany

Salem

Pittsfield

Massachusetts

Boston

Northampton

Worcester

Brockton

Springfield

Plymouth

Providence

Hartford

Rhode Island

Connecticut

Norwich

Newport

New Haven

New London

Southampton

Hudson

Puritan
New England

By contrast, religion stood at the heart of the New England enterprise. The first colony (1620) was the Plymouth Plantation of the Pilgrims, who were intent on separating spiritually as well as physically from the Church of England. The second, and far more influential, was the "Puritan" colony of Massachusetts Bay, founded in 1629. In the next thirteen years, some 20,000 souls crossed from England to Massachusetts in what became known as the "Great Migration." Some moved on to the Hartford and New Haven colonies that merged into Connecticut; others migrated north to New Hampshire and the eventual state of Maine. Some moved to Rhode Island to protest religious rules. Puritans did not intend to leave the Church of England but to reform it from within and to establish a godly society in the process. Both could happen more easily, they thought, on a distant shore than amid England's turbulence. But memories of home inevitably shaped the way they understood church and society. Many of them came from the region of East Anglia, thick with towns and commerce and ministers drawn from the Puritan stronghold of Cambridge University. They represented the radical end of England's long and winding Reformation.

Protestantism was established in England as an act of state stemming from King Henry VIII's determination to sire a legitimate son, and to go through wives until he got one. When the pope refused to let him out of his first marriage, Henry took England out of the Roman Catholic Church instead. But both he and Queen Elizabeth I, by far the ablest of his offspring, wanted to keep the Reformation moderate. In particular, they wanted to retain a formal liturgy and a hierarchy of bishops. More zealous Protestants insisted on a thorough "purification" (hence, Puritan) of such "popish" elements. Through Elizabeth's reign and that of her successor, James I, however, they were often stymied in getting their way in the church at large. They settled for developing informal networks of likeminded churches in which self-selected, highly committed members shared plain-style worship centered on the preaching of Scripture and strict Reformed theology. This accommodation ended under Charles I, whose archbishop, William Laud, insisted on conformity to the prayer book. When Charles began to rule without consent of Parliament, and when economic hard times descended, some of the Puritan party determined to move to America to flee the wrath to come. More positively, they hoped to establish pure churches, a society run by biblical standards, a constitutional government, and a chance at prosperity for themselves and their children. They hoped to construct a model that they could re-export to England come judgment day.

These high ideals contained tensions that erupted in the very first decade of settlement, as once-rebels in old England became the establishment in New. Roger

Williams, pastor at Salem, protested that a truly pure church could not take charge of public space as Massachusetts aimed to do. Williams was banished when he refused to conform. He then founded Rhode Island on his alternative principles, and it became the haven of New England dissent. Anne Hutchinson, a midwife and Bible-study leader of considerable theological expertise, made similar arguments with respect to salvation. The pastors of Massachusetts tried to comfort troubled souls—and promote social harmony—by treating godly behavior as possible evidence of true faith. This, Anne charged, was a gospel of good works rather than the Protestant principle of grace alone. The authorities worried that such open dissent could damage the delicate state of their new colony and so ordered Anne to be silent. When she refused, she too was banished and died in an Indian conflict on Long Island. Her lineage came back to haunt Boston in the person of Thomas Hutchinson, Loyalist Lieutenant Governor in the years before the Revolution.

After this rocky start, New England settled down to a steady, stable course of development. Its town and family pattern of settlement was crucial. Far fewer single young men drifted ashore here than in the Chesapeake; rather, families with some capital in hand set up family farms aimed at modest returns over the long run. These families, moreover, gathered in towns rather than dispersing to separate plantations. Family heads "covenanted" together upon arrival, creating consensual communities for common purposes. The most important common goals were establishing a church and conducting land sales. Newcomers had to sign on to this covenant and so were absorbed into established webs of regulated relationships. Even if committed Puritans constituted only about twenty percent of the settlers, church attendance was mandatory. Everyone was to live under one sacred canopy by one set of ethical norms.

In Massachusetts, voting in colony-wide elections was restricted to men who had met the high bar of full church membership. This included presenting a convincing narrative of their personal conversion experience. In local town meetings, however, voting was open to almost all adult males. The aim of such "democracy" was, again, to maximize consent to mutual obligations and to minimize dissent going forward. Finally, each town was mandated to support a school to instruct both girls and boys in basic literacy. As ultra-Protestants, the Puritans demanded a population that was able to read the Bible, and to guide that reading they mandated an educated clergy. Harvard College was founded for that purpose in 1636, seven years after first settlement. Virginia took twelve times as long to charter its first college, William and Mary.

Minister, magistrate, and schoolmaster thus represented the stable tripod of New England society. It rested upon a floor of widespread property ownership. The climate and soil of New England did not make for large plantations raising commodities for export. Instead, modest-size farms that produced grains, meat, and dairy dominated the countryside. Craftspeople and stores in town supplied additional needs. Surplus crops were carted to the ports along the New England coast to feed the sugar islands in the Caribbean. This commerce would become more and more important to the New England economy as the tide of new immigrants—and needy customers—tapered off after 1642, when civil war broke out in England. Merchants became more cosmopolitan as they sought out trade beyond home-grown goods. Some ports were completely independent of the farm economy and had little or no tie to Puritan ways of life. Gloucester's profane fishermen prospered as they exported cod back to a hungry Europe. Newport became the capital of the North American slave trade, despite the devotion to (religious) liberty on which Rhode Island was founded. If New England had very modest numbers of enslaved Africans—house-servants for the elite, dock-workers in Boston—its economy was thickly intertwined with the slave-labor colonies of the Caribbean and southern mainland.

At home, however, New Englanders had reason to thank the God upon whose promises they banked. They created the healthiest, most fertile and literate place in the Western world. It had one of the highest percentages of college-educated leadership in American history. It could claim the highest rates of active participation in church and state, and the lowest rates of crime and slavery, in the Western Hemisphere. Social trust was very high. So was social homogeneity. After 1642, immigration into New England stayed low for 200 years, until refugees from the Irish potato famine poured ashore in the 1840s. Until then the majority of New Englanders descended from the 20,000 people who had arrived in the "Great Migration." Ethnically, they were more English than England itself, which in these years was absorbing Irish, Scots, and French Huguenots by the thousands. In short, New England had the dynamics of a vast extended family. Its crisis moments erupted just there.

THE DEFINING CRISES

The most predictable problems involved "outsiders." Like Virginia, New England had its own early conflict with Indians, the Pequot War of 1637. It proved especially murderous because the colonists deliberately attacked the stockades where the native women and children huddled (as they thought) out of harm's way. This was the only way that whites knew to draw native warriors out of the forest to fight them on their own terms. As Puritans they also had the Hebrews' conquest of Canaan as a model, complete with examples of extermination. After this early crisis, New England had fairly smooth sailing for forty years. Then in 1675 tensions over land and trade, driven by acute population growth, exploded into King Philip's War. This was, proportionate to population, one of the costliest wars in American history; one half of the white towns were attacked and one third of the native population died in the fray. This time the troubles did not end when the war ended. Another outsider, King James II, in 1686 combined the New England colonies with his own province of New York and annulled their charters in the process. The worst consequences were prevented when the pro-Catholic king ran afoul of Parliament, which agreed to the invasion of England by William of Orange. This "Glorious Revolution" solved a long-term political problem at home and tried to do so in New England. Massachusetts's new charter ended the "rule of the regenerate" by making property, not piety, the criterion for voting in colony-wide elections.

On top of all this, war broke out again on the New England frontier in 1688, part of the Anglo-French conflict in Europe. The stage was set for the Salem witch craze. Along with Thanksgiving, this is the one episode most Americans think they know about New England history. Indeed, many times more books have been written about the case than the number of casualties it claimed. For our purposes, we can view it as the way a tightly-wound community might respond to overwhelming stresses from without and within. Their ministers had been warning New Englanders for decades that God was getting impatient with their supposed failure to live up to their covenant with him. When evils mounted despite rituals of reform and repentance, attacking *inside* evildoers seemed the solution. They were all in the family. The first accusers of witchcraft were young girls just coming into womanhood. The typical accused was a single woman past childbearing years who sometimes had economic independence besides. Further, the tide of accusations swelled right after Salem took in refugees fleeing the war zone in Maine. They arrived with horror stories of Indian massacres and kidnappings prompted by French (Catholic) instigators. Thirdly, the accusers were more associated with the traditional farm economy, the accused with the rising mercantile system. Behind the scenes, finally, lay old grievances within the church. Rival families had been quarreling for years at Salem over their preferred pastors, opening a crevasse across this supposedly firm foundation of the community. Ordinarily, the magistrates quashed witch-hunting panics, but in this case they were overwhelmed by the recent cascade of problems. They put an end to things only after twenty victims had been killed and scores more imprisoned.

LASTING LEGACIES

When the wars with France finally ceased in 1715, the North Atlantic world entered into twenty-five years of remarkable growth and prosperity. New England shared in this but far less than did the colonies to its south. The ports of New York City and Philadelphia outmatched Boston. Virginia, Pennsylvania, and New York had vast interiors for new settlement, while New England was blocked from expansion anywhere but the unpromising frontier of Vermont and Maine. The return of war in the 1740s again hit New England first before migrating south, and the widows, orphans, and debts it left behind put serious strains upon the colonies' budgets. New England almost unanimously favored the War for Independence and opposed the War of 1812, so suffered less internal strife than did other regions. But its future in 1815 looked to be landlocked and declining. This hardly seemed the region poised to define the identity and mission of the new country.

Salvation appeared in the form of one of American history's most important public works projects, the Erie Canal. It connected the Great Lakes with the Atlantic Ocean and provided a route for pent-up New Englanders to pour out across New York and the Upper Midwest. They took along the schools, churches, community consciousness, and zeal to build in this new "wilderness" the holy commonwealth their ancestors had attempted two centuries before. Once again their efforts showed the old Puritan oscillation between radicalism and order. On the one hand, the New England diaspora provided the bedrock of the Whig and Republican parties across the upper North. On the other hand, it also provided leaders and foot-soldiers in the crusades for Prohibition, abolition, feminism, utopian communes, and radical religion.

John Winthrop, the first governor of Massachusetts Bay, had cautioned his settlers that they would be "a citty

on a hill." God was giving them a test that, were they faith-
ful and brave, they might pass. But they also might fail.
Every fifty years or so the heirs of his people went through
a collective crisis over how they were measuring up. In the
1850s it was a fond chronicler of New England ways, Har-
riet Beecher Stowe, who pushed the question hard in *Uncle
Tom's Cabin*. In 1861 the Boston activist Julia Ward Howe
answered with hope and triumph in "The Battle Hymn of
the Republic." For the next hundred years the song stood
as the American anthem of righteous aspiration.

5

The Middle Colonies

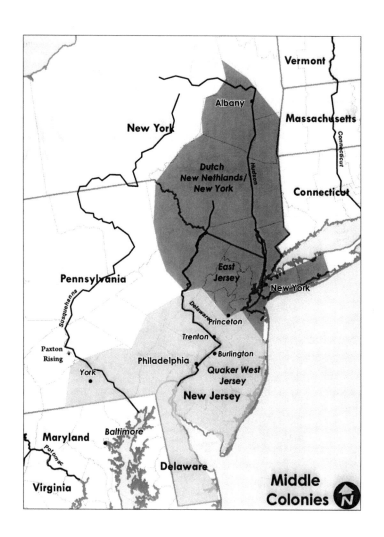

Vermont

New York

Albany

Massachusetts

Connecticut

Dutch
New Nethlands/
New York

Hudson

Connecticut

East
Jersey

Pennsylvania

Susquehanna

New York

Delaware

Princeton

Trenton

Paxton
Rising

Burlington

York

Philadelphia

Quaker West
Jersey

New Jersey

Maryland

Baltimore

Potomac

Delaware

Virginia

Middle
Colonies
N

If New England made up the most homogenous region, the Middle Colonies, immediately to its south, were the most diverse. New Netherland, founded in 1614, set the pattern. A good half of its early population was not Dutch, and a visitor in 1644 was told that eighteen languages could be heard on the streets of Manhattan. Things got more complicated when England seized the colony in 1664. The Duke of York (later the ill-fated King James II) named it after his title and ruled it from abroad through personally appointed governors. The Dutch retained rights to their language and church, but English and Anglicanism were now in the driver's seat. Meanwhile, English of the Puritan sort crossed from Connecticut to plant settlements on Long Island. The pattern repeated in the divided land that would become New Jersey. East (we would call it north) Jersey saw both Anglicans and Dutch Reformed come over from New York, but another resettlement from Connecticut (at Newark) plus Baptists and Quakers direct from England and then Scots Presbyterians made this a true hodge-podge. West (south) Jersey belonged to an investment company run by Quakers, so more of that group settled there but many of the others as well.

A similar situation existed in the much larger Pennsylvania, province of the radical—and pacifist—son and namesake of William Penn, an admiral who had ably served both Oliver Cromwell and Charles II. In 1681, Charles paid his debts to the Penn family by giving the younger Penn rights to the lands between New York and Maryland, with present-day Delaware in the bargain. William made it into a haven for his fellow Quakers but was also determined to rescue the family fortunes, for he had run up debts of his own. Religious conviction and profit combined; Pennsylvania became a pioneer of free conscience and real-estate promotion. Penn sent agents to the Rhine Valley, which was caught up in the perennial wars of King Louis XIV of France. Members of German "peace churches" like the Amish and Mennonites were especially quick to respond to his offer of cheap land. These "Deutsch" became the "Pennsylvania Dutch."

They would be succeeded in the eighteenth century by thousands of Germans from the established Lutheran and Reformed churches, and some Catholics, too. Overlapping with this tide but then, after the 1750s, far outpacing it was an influx of people of Scots descent, some directly from the Lowlands, others who had migrated to the north of Ireland. These Protestant "Ulstermen" (after that northern Irish county) counted themselves as Irish, but Americans would re-label them "Scots-Irish" to distinguish them from the Catholics in the south of the island. While some of these Scots-Irish settled in the seacoast cities, the majority headed west to the Appalachian frontier. We will examine them there in the next chapter.

In short, the Middle Colonies made up a patchwork

quilt. What were the stitches that kept it together? The first set was a robust market economy based on family farms like New England's, only on better soil. The ample surpluses were shipped by better river transportation to larger ports. By the 1700s, the Middle Colonies had become the breadbasket of North America and the Caribbean's largest food source. From that trade Philadelphia and New York built the shipping, insurance, and small-shop manufacturing services that made them colonial America's largest cities. After two hundred years' experience to the contrary since Columbus's landfall, the Middle Colonies demonstrated that substantial wealth could be generated in the Western Hemisphere under a largely free-labor system. Largely. Many Germans arrived in Pennsylvania as "redemptioners" who owed labor for their passage, but unlike the Chesapeake's indentured servants, they often had family and ethnic ties that improved their chances.

Meanwhile, the big ports depended on enslaved Africans to work the docks and shops. Here emerged a third model of life and labor under bondage in contrast to those of the Chesapeake and Lower South. The city offered more variety and mobility than did southern plantations, but the lower number of Africans in the North forced quicker assimilation and fewer possibilities in terms of marriage partners and social networks. The black communities in Northern cities did hold their own festivals once a year on which, for one day, they defied slavery's constraints. In Boston this was Election Day; in New York it was "Pinkster" (Dutch Pentecost). They elected their own leaders and conducted parades and parties in African style in which they parodied white roles of wealth and power. Overall, however, slavery in the Middle Colonies did not extend much beyond the cities and some big Dutch estates in the Hudson Valley.

The second set of stitches lay in the religious denomination, a key American innovation. In Europe a single church typically held official status in a given territory. Even if other fellowships might be tolerated, this body could think of itself as the one true church. The variety of the Middle Colonies made that a non-starter. Each group might still insist that theirs was the *best* church but not the only one. They had to recognize their neighbors as genuine Christians, not try to shut them down. Their real challenge lay in binding their scattered congregations into a network that maintained consistent doctrine and practice across long distances in a strange environment. While the Mennonites and Amish immigrated along tight kinship lines, and Roman Catholics clustered together as a suspect minority, people of Lutheran and Calvinist background often drifted in and about more individually. Their churches helped gather them in and settle them down, providing familiar grounds of culture and language. Denominations emerged to connect these local communities over a terrain that stretched from the Hudson to the Delaware, and from ocean to mountains.

Religion and ethnicity translated into politics, too.

Here lay the roots of another American invention, the political party. The shape of governance in other regions—the planter hierarchy to the south and the homogenous towns to the north—did not fit a patchwork society. Instead, each local group had to determine who were their friends and enemies across the colony. Their leaders, gathering in the capital to do business, then forged loose coalitions with their allies to outmaneuver their foes. Over time these coalitions firmed up into permanent camps: the Livingston faction versus the De Lanceys' in New York, the Quaker party centered in the Assembly versus the Proprietary party around the governor in Pennsylvania. The results looked all too modern: constant squabbling, backroom dealing, and the raw assertion of self-interest over against any sense of a common good. The first political parties in the new United States had their roots and chieftains in New York City: Alexander Hamilton for the Federalists against Aaron Burr, Jr. for the Democratic-Republicans. They pursued their battle to their final, fatal duel across the Hudson in New Jersey.

Furthermore, political success depended on currying favor abroad. The Middle Colonies had all been founded as proprietorships. In this arrangement the Crown assigned control over a territory to a single individual or small group of wealthy investors who would bear the expense of settling immigrants in hopes of garnering a profit. Much more than in Virginia or New England, therefore, considerable power remained with elites back in England. In the case of Pennsylvania, these were the heirs of William Penn; in New York it was the Crown itself. The proprietors appointed governors to do their bidding. These were almost always outsiders holding powerful executive authority but parachuted into unfamiliar circumstances. Predictably, their offices became centers—and objects— of jostling and intrigue. Eventually, the elected assemblies started sending representatives of their own back to England to lobby the proprietor—or his enemies, and/or the king, and/or parliament—directly.

Benjamin Franklin was the most famous lobbyist, and perhaps the representative man of the Middle Colonies as a whole. He arrived in Philadelphia as an outsider, having been born and reared in Boston. He became one of America's richest men owing to his enterprising spirit and political connections as a commercial printer. At mid-life, as a wealthy man, he took up a second career in public service. He envisioned a time when the colonies would come to equal the mother country in population and wealth, and perhaps hoped to become His Majesty's first prime minister for America. First, however, he was the Pennsylvania Assembly's lobbyist in London, promoting their goal of having Pennsylvania taken away from the Penns and made a royal colony. That is, until shortly before the Revolution, Franklin and the Quaker party behind him wanted not less but more royal rule. Patchwork politics majored in paradox, complexity, and irony.

THE DEFINING CRISIS

Conflict was built into such a diverse society, and periodically it boiled over into violence. New York City whites panicked over an alleged "great Negro plot" in 1741. Through executions and exile to the Caribbean, this occasioned many more casualties than did the infamous episode at Salem, but it did not expose a fundamental conflict in values. The Paxton uprising on the Pennsylvania frontier in 1763 did, but grew out of the dynamics of the backcountry and so will be treated in the next section. The Middle Colonies met their crisis in the War for Independence itself. Here the American Revolution was truly a civil war. No colonies had greater proportions of Loyalists or turned out so many combatants on both sides of the conflict. The ethno-religious factions raised their game to higher stakes. Pennsylvania's Quakers stayed loyal or neutral, both for pacifist and commercial reasons. The Amish and Mennonites tried to stay out of harm's way. The Lutherans, German Reformed, and Presbyterians supported independence and seized power from the Quaker-led establishment. They imposed severe wartime constraints on their opponents and passed the most revolutionary constitution of all the thirteen new states. In New York and New Jersey the Dutch Reformed split, the more evangelical tending Patriot, the more traditional either neutral or Loyalist. Anglicans divided, too. The more urban and elite sided with Britain, the commoners were Patriots or neutrals. The ironic close-up once again belongs to Benjamin Franklin. Before the war, he had his son William installed as royal governor of New Jersey. When the troubles started, William remained loyal to the king. Benjamin endorsed his imprisonment for the duration of the war. The two never reconciled.

Ultimately, armies on the ground decided matters. Many locals took up arms for Britain when its troops marched through the neighborhood. But once these had left, Patriot bands took over and took vengeance on those who had aided the British. Philadelphia provided warm hospitality to British General William Howe over the winter of 1777–78 while the Patriots' Continental Army suffered at nearby Valley Forge. But when Howe left the next spring, so did the Loyalists' hopes. New York City served as Britain's permanent base from the moment in autumn 1776 when George Washington nearly lost the Revolution by trying to defend the city. The last battle in the region was fought to a draw at Monmouth, New Jersey in the spring of 1778, on the British army's march back to New York from Philadelphia. After that, Washington stayed encamped at Morristown and the British in New York City. The war in the Middle Colonies literally ended in stalemate. When the British fleet finally sailed from New York in 1783, it took along some five hundred Loyalist families. In all 60,000 Loyalists left their homeland. Relative to population, this was a larger train of émigrés than fled the French Revolution or the Vietnam War.

LASTING LEGACIES

The region's long-term legacy to the nation shows some overlap with the other sections' but finally falls along different lines. Like Virginia, New York has contributed notable political leaders—Civil War Secretary of State William Seward, Grover Cleveland, and the two presidents Roosevelt. But New Jersey's Woodrow Wilson really came from Virginia, and Pennsylvania, for all its status as the original "keystone state," has produced only one president, James Buchanan. He is arguably the greatest failure ever to hold that office. Likewise, the region features notable colleges and universities, but it did not forge the nation's religion, academy, and literature as New England did. In the twentieth century, New York City did become the nation's cultural capital, but much of its talent flocked there from other places.

The Middle Atlantic instead has distinguished itself as America's commercial leader. Wall Street stands for big finance, Madison Avenue for advertising, 30 Rock for the great radio and television networks. New York and Philadelphia were the nation's first cities of international trade and the homes of the great railroads and their titans: Vanderbilt, Harriman, and the Pennsylvania line. New York City is also the emblem of cosmopolitanism and diversity. At Castle Garden and Ellis Island, tens of millions of European immigrants came ashore. Harlem stands for urban African-America with all its music, literature, and churches. Likewise, the Lower East Side means immigrant Jewish culture.

In short, Quaker Pennsylvania's original formula has spread its magic across the rest of the nation. Property rights, trade, tolerance, and diversity bring prosperity, turbulence, and creative adaptation. The upshot is Benjamin Franklin's rough pragmatism, which avoids high principles but enables people to get on with life. It is fitting that he helped craft the federal Constitution in Philadelphia and could see George Washington inaugurated president on Wall Street.

6

The
Backcountry

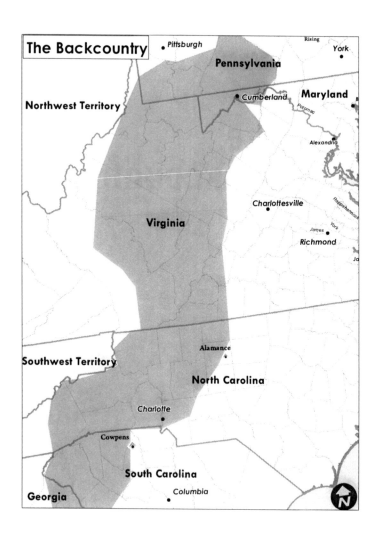

The Backcountry

Pittsburgh

Rising

York

Pennsylvania

Northwest Territory

Cumberland

Maryland

B

Potomac

Alexandria

Charlottesville

Rappahannock

Virginia

James

York

Richmond

Ja

Alamance

Southwest Territory

North Carolina

Charlotte

Cowpens

South Carolina

Columbia

Georgia

N

Benjamin Franklin groused about all the German he heard on the streets of Philadelphia and wondered if authorities should impose an English-only policy. As it turned out, his values were more challenged by the group that arrived on the heels of the Germans, the Scots-Irish. The label technically applies to Protestants whose ancestors had migrated from Scotland to the north of Ireland, but in America it also came to cover immigrants from the northern counties of England and the adjacent Scottish Lowlands. An amazing 250,000 of them arrived in the American colonies between 1720 and 1775, first of all at Philadelphia. Some lingered there, but most proceeded west until they hit the Appalachian range. They migrated along those mountains to fill the backcountry of Pennsylvania, Virginia, and the Carolinas. They set the image of American frontier people, celebrated in popular lore but called by more telling nicknames up close: Hoosiers and Jayhawks, crackers and rednecks. In Franklin's time it was more often "ruffians" or "rough-scuff." The first president born out of this stream was Andrew Jackson.

This people's edgy personality grew out of their place in British history. England and Scotland fought over their borderlands for centuries, leaving government there shallow and unsettled. Since the authorities were more likely to be foreigners than neighbors, the inhabitants turned for security to family networks. They also cultivated a prickly code of honor that promised violent retribution to threats real or imagined. Better to head off violence, they figured, before it began. Their land being more suited to grazing than farming, people learned to live light and mobile. Traditional farming did work better in some parts of the Scottish Lowlands, but there over-population became a problem in the seventeenth century. London concocted a brilliant solution. This moderately suspect people would be transplanted to Northern Ireland ("Ulster") to occupy lands seized from a more troublesome lot, rebellious Roman Catholics. Relief for Scotland would spell better security for England and make Northern Ireland into a profitable trading partner in the bargain. London particularly encouraged flax and linen production there to drive down the competition England felt from Irish wool. On the ground, this meant that in Ireland hard-pressed Scots became tenants of absentee English magnates as a bulwark against dispossessed natives, demeaned as Gaelic-speaking "savages." In religious terms, the Presbyterian worship of the Ulsterites was tolerated by an Anglican establishment as a superior alternative to the superstitious Irish "papists." All in all, the transplanted Scots became border people once again.

Once the French wars ended (in 1715), the predictable consequences began. As their leases came due, the Ulsterites found their rents "racked" up by distant English landlords. When their sons angled for a way up—in the officer corps or at university—they were barred for being Presbyterian. When it came time to export their linen, London manipulated the trade for English gain. Waves of emigration ensued, at such a volume that some local authorities worried that the countryside would be deserted. But that did not change policy, and the waves continued. Fully half of the quarter million who went to America did so in the last decade before independence, 1765–1775. Just as American politics heated up over tensions with Great Britain, the mass of Scots-Irish complicated things even more.

In migrating to the frontier, the Scots-Irish were opting for the familiar. Here were mountains and foothills like those of the borderlands. The terrain was made for grazing and light agriculture, for frequent moves and spare living. Government was far away, kin close at hand. Rivalries over land and status were acute and settled man to man. Although the people were materially poor, they treasured their self-respect. If freedom became a word for nothing left to lose, it was far better than servility. Promises of money and security from the powerful usually proved to be false; better to maintain one's integrity and independence instead. These lessons of the past seemed all the more relevant in the new country, for once again the Scots-Irish found themselves on the border. The "heathen savages" were not Irish Roman Catholics. Now they were the native peoples to the west. The Anglo magnates didn't live in London. Now they were the merchants, bankers, and government officials to the east. They controlled the terms of trade and got to certify land titles. Their agents moved in after the Scots-Irish had begun to develop a mountain tract. They demanded rent—or threatened eviction—in the name of a rich planter like George Washington or a businessman like Benjamin Franklin. In fact, Washington and Franklin alone speculated in western lands to the tune of hundreds of thousands of acres. When the powerful finally demanded too much, or delivered too little, the backcountry rose up, armed and dangerous.

Such were the "Regulation" movements that arose in the western counties of North and South Carolina in the late 1760s. Regulators were voluntary bands of citizens who held no office but maintained a vigilant watch (hence, "vigilante") to enforce traditional community standards of justice and fair play. When they saw these violated, they petitioned colonial officials for quick redress—or else. In North Carolina, the complaints alleged a crushing weight of taxes that supported extravagant government spending (on an opulent new governor's mansion in particular). Even worse, a cabal of sheriffs and recently arrived lawyers from the east coast were said to be engaged in legal shenanigans to seize the farms of ordinary people. When their complaints went unheeded, North Carolina's Regulators shut down county courts, prompting the governor to mobilize the militia. The two sides met in pitched battle at Alamance Creek in May 1771, with the militia quickly routing the rebels. Six leading Regulators were tried and hanged; others had their properties seized. Some moved further west. When the Revolution came, these Regulators joined those who had stayed behind and formed a hard core of Loyalist support. The Patriots in this case turned out to be the elite.

In South Carolina the complaints were the opposite, that there was too *little* law. This stemmed from the Low Country planters' keeping all power centralized in Charleston. The resulting story is familiar from a hundred Hollywood Westerns. The Regulators represented the "good people" of the frontier angered by marauding bands of gunmen who raided, raped, and rustled with impunity. Taking the law into their own hands, the Regulators captured the bandits and tried them in makeshift tribunals. Finally, the authorities in the capital started paying attention. The Assembly voted to extend the court system to the backcountry to make order and prosperity secure for all. During the Revolution these Regulators proved to be firm Patriots.

Among their Loyalist opponents were recently arrived Scots Highlanders who bore some old, familiar enmities. Catholic in religion and long loyal to the House of Stuart, they had arisen to support "Bonnie Prince" Charles Stuart's bid for the throne in 1745. When he was defeated, by ancient custom they transferred their allegiance to the Crown. When rebels in their new North American neighborhood rose against the king, the Highlanders flocked to his banner. The religious factor—old Catholics vs.

ultra-Protestant Scots-Irish—intensified the fighting. The Revolution reached its bloodiest peak as a civil war in the backcountry of the Lower South, partly because its pattern and grievances were so old as well as so fresh.

THE DEFINING CRISIS

The single most vicious incident, however, happened on the frontier of Pennsylvania, in the "Paxton Boys'" slaughter of Christianized Indians in late 1763. Here the bill of Pennsylvania's dual principles came due. The colony had been founded on the promise of peace and fair dealings with the Indians, but also on the need for land sales to relieve the Penn family's financial woes. Once its reputation as a small farmer's paradise got out, the pressure on the frontier grew unrelenting. The colony took in people of any and all conviction, including Scots-Irish pioneers who hardly shared Quaker commitments to pacifism. The Quakers tried to handle the problem by flagrant gerrymandering. The majority of the Assembly were elected from eastern districts, leaving the western population grossly underrepresented. Matters came to a head in the French and Indian War, which began in Pennsylvania's backyard and boiled on there for years, at high costs of death and refugees.

When violence flared up again in 1763 in a pan-Indian offensive named after the Odawa leader Pontiac, the Scots-Irish of Paxton Township (near Lancaster) fought back. No one else would, they complained. During the recent war Philadelphia had knuckled under to Quaker opinion and had underfunded military protection on the frontier. Now it was happening again. The Paxton Boys turned on a peaceful settlement of Conestoga Indians, wiped out as many as they could, then staged a follow-up raid two weeks later to kill the rest. Next they organized a march on Philadelphia to eliminate the Indians being harbored there and to demand due protection from the colonial government. Benjamin Franklin led a militia (which included some armed Quakers, the protestors quickly noted) to confront the marchers outside of town and managed to defuse the situation. That did not keep him from entering fully into the ensuing war of words, in which he called the Indians far better Christians than the white savages who claimed the name. After redistricting, however, the balance in the Assembly changed, and Franklin found it easier take up imperial diplomacy in London than to remain in Pennsylvania.

LASTING LEGACIES

Leaving the record just with conflict and violence would be unfair, as the Scots-Irish themselves have argued over the years. In fact, they have left an outsized imprint on American culture, high and low. On the elite level, the Presbyterian commitment to higher education, along with Scotland's foremost place in the eighteenth-century

Enlightenment, combined to sow academies all along the frontier. Hampden-Sydney, Washington and Lee, and Washington and Jefferson are among the colleges and universities that stem from these academies. At the same time, Northern British custom took haunts and dreams very seriously as auguries for this world and communications from the next. The backcountry thus became a place of lively visionary culture right next to, and opposite of, the rational book learning of the academies.

A most familiar American religious ritual came out of this setting, too. In Scotland, rural Presbyterians observed the custom of "holy fairs." People flocked from miles around to hold multi-day outdoor assemblies where earnest preachers exhorted them to repent of their sins. Those who did would conclude the meeting by sharing the Lord's Supper. In the American backcountry this morphed into camp-meetings and the fires of frontier revivalism. The music heard there and at more secular entertainments seeded the Appalachian style that went national with the advent of radio. By the late twentieth century, it had become the pop-culture powerhouse of country music. By then two other juggernauts had rolled down out of the same hills. Pentecostal religion, defined by visions, miracles, and speaking in tongues, grew over the twentieth century into a major force in American Christianity, and even more around the world. Meanwhile, stock-car racing turned into a premier American sport. The Triple Crown of thoroughbred horse racing remained for Tidewater blue-bloods; the dirt track of motorized steel led back into the hills.

Education, religion, music, sports—and politics. From the death of John Kennedy to the election of Barack Obama, every occupant of the White House except for the accidental Gerald Ford hailed from the Southern-to-Far-Western band known as the Sunbelt. This was the great arc to which millions had migrated out of the old backcountry. All its presidents—the Democrats Johnson, Carter, and Clinton; the Republicans Reagan and both Bushes—learned to speak its accents and sound its values. On the current scene, the old map of backcountry settlement coincides exactly with the map showing Donald Trump's strongest support.

7

Conclusion

WEAVING THE STORIES TOGETHER

Let's return to the observation we made at the start of this book. History tries to weave a story out of piles of data from the past to help us understand what happened back then and make better sense of our lives today. But we have put five stories on the table, leaving us with two questions: How did they all come together? And how do they—separately and together—help us live with a little more wisdom and understanding in our own times?

Answering the first question fully would lead us into all the twists and turns of American history down to the present moment. Here's a very short sketch. Once the Patriots had outlasted the British in the War for Independence, the new United States tried briefly to live under the Articles of Confederation, which allowed a great deal of state (and therefore, regional) autonomy. Within a few years, some powerful leaders decided that the ship of state needed a tighter set of rules. The result was the Constitution compiled at a convention that met behind closed doors over a long, hot Philadelphia summer in 1787. Several key calculations went into its construction. Two are well known: the compromise between large and small states, and the compromise over slavery. A third compromise involved a regional deal.

The leading designers of the Constitution came from Virginia, New York, and Pennsylvania. They thought they had a lot in common. Slavery seemed to be on the way out in the Chesapeake because raising tobacco proved to be so hard on the soil. Planters like George Washington were going over to grain agriculture, which didn't need slaves. So the Virginia delegates thought that their state would become more and more like Pennsylvania, with a vast spread of farms serviced by some coastal ports. These states together would form a solid middle bloc between the extremists to the north and to the south, between the religious radicals of New England and the devotees of slavery in the Lower South. Plus, the Virginia delegates believed that their river, the Potomac, would become the main highway into the new nation's vast interior. The national capital would be placed on its banks, and down its waters would flow the produce of the agricultural hinterland. Put in regional terms, the South would tether the West into a farm-based majority coalition that kept the commercial Northeast—New England and New York—in check.

That arrangement worked for a long time. The Chesapeake and its diaspora across Kentucky and Tennessee dominated the presidency, the Supreme Court, and the Senate into the 1850s. They did so with the support of the lower North—Pennsylvania and the states just north of the Ohio River. Slavery did not fade away but expanded via highly profitable cotton agriculture from the Lower South to the Mississippi River. The Chesapeake planters wove themselves to this system by selling off thousands of their enslaved young people to work the new plantations. But up North the Erie Canal symbolized a rival new alliance. The "West" that the Founders had envisioned divided into two, and its upper part affiliated with the Northeast. Family farms, bustling commerce, and new industry spread from New England and New York across the Midwest. New immigrants poured in from Europe for opportunities in this growing economy. The whole system was premised on free movement of free labor with massive government aid to business and industry. The Southern alliance demanded the opposite. The tensions between the two sides finally exploded when Abraham Lincoln was elected president. His election depended on Pennsylvania's move from its long alliance with Virginia in the Democratic Party over to the Republican column.

The North's victory in the Civil War sealed its dominance in the nation for the next hundred years. At the time it seemed so natural, as if things had always been this way and would always remain so. But they hadn't been and wouldn't be. The 1960s seemed to spell the triumph of the North's progressive liberalism but in fact set in motion the triumph of a new coalition between South and West. Commentators called it Sunbelt conservativism. The success of the civil rights movement made the old South respectable again. The spread of air-conditioning made it habitable. Massive government investments in military bases and industries from World War II through the Cold

War triggered an economic boom across the region. The "Sunbelt" was also the "Gunbelt." The result was a vast population shift from north and east to south and west. In the presidential election of 1940, the old slave states plus the modern West held a minority 247 of the nation's 531 electoral votes. By 2000, they controlled a majority 313 of 538. Among the migrants were George Bush, father and son, who left New England for Texas, and Ronald Reagan, who moved from Illinois to California. They eventually landed in the White House to support a political program hospitable to their adopted homes.

TAKEAWAYS FOR TODAY

How our different stories come together, then, continues to be a work in progress. *E pluribus unum* remains a goal, but we shouldn't be too surprised when it doesn't match up with reality. Given the variety built into the origins of the United States, it could hardly be otherwise. To repeat what we said at the start, the United States was not born out of a golden age of harmony and peace. The first settlers argued with each other. The War for Independence was a civil war. The members of the Philadelphia convention that wrote the Constitution took forever to settle their differences. The Constitution itself was ratified by specially elected assemblies, but it probably would not have won a direct popular vote. People today, therefore, should not berate themselves or each other for being quarrelsome. We should ponder instead what we are quarreling about and how. We should ponder how the Founders of the country managed to come together over all their differences to create a workable consensus and a working system. We should ponder just as much how resolute idealists pushed against some parts of that consensus, especially slavery, and carried on decade after decade, seemingly against all odds, to see their cause through to ultimate success.

That success was not complete, of course. Emancipation did not end racial inequality and injustice; it did not obliterate the racism that was invented to justify American slavery in the first place. When we think back on early American history and how important slave labor was to the foundations and continuing operations of the economy for two hundred years, we can see a debt unpaid as well as a wound unhealed. People may differ on how to provide recompense and healing. We cannot deny our obligation to do so. And we cannot hear the celebrated keywords of the American story—liberty and equality, chosen nation, promised land—without hearing the dissonant chords that history adds to the mix. This is not to cynically dismiss the ideals, but rather, to take them as a calling instead of as an accomplishment.

Our tour of early America also reveals how much each of those systems of life and values still endures today—not just in different regions or the nation as a whole, but in each one of us. Who does not resonate to the image of the New England town meeting or that region's legacy in religion, education, and culture? Who does not honor the Middle Colonies' pluralism and enterprise or (wish to) benefit from the prosperity it birthed? Leadership with a sense of command *and* of responsibility to the public good as the best of the Chesapeake gentry showed—who does not want that for their country and community? The Lower South sets the stage for the redemption of suffering, both for the African arrivals on its shore and the Ulster pilgrims of its backcountry. The Scots-Irish struggle between a rock and a hard place, the pride and resilience of making your own way—these have entered deeply into the common experience and the sacred mythology of the American people. We might find ourselves to be more the heirs of one of these stories than of another, but we also have taken on some of them all. We feel the riches and also the tensions of this inheritance. Walt Whitman, one of America's greatest poets, put it this way in his "Song of Myself," which is really the tableau of a nation:

> Do I contradict myself?
> Very well then I contradict myself,
> (I am large, I contain multitudes.)

Our tensions do not arise simply from one region's legacy rubbing against another's. Each story had a "defining crisis" because each region—between its value system, its economy, its way of life, and its development over time—harbored interior tensions that came to an explosion. Our problems don't arise just from outsiders but from within ourselves. Here history best serves its role as "a distant mirror." Seeing the forces and aspirations that drove other people to a moment of truth surely can prompt us to some reflection and self-recognition. We can more easily consider the shadow side of our own aspirations, examine where the logic of our life will lead us, contemplate not just the things outside our reach but the curse of answered prayer. The study of history does not promise to solve our problems but can help us discern what our problems really are, where they come from, and how we have helped bring them on ourselves.

TWO MORE TAKEAWAYS

It is not just Americans who can profit from thinking about early America. These colonies made up an emerging society par excellence, with fragile political systems and multiple groups trying to find their way. The United States today may look like a giant astride the world, but it got there from some very rudimentary beginnings and against the conventional wisdom that such a society would never work. Europeans sniped that North America was a barbaric shore, that anyone who went there lost whatever civilized mind and morals they might possess. Without excusing everything that the United States has done, at home or abroad, we can surely find that judgment to have been mistaken. So also with emerging nations around the globe today. Poverty, social unrest, and political discord tend to dominate Western news reportage of these locales, but people there can take heart, and some instruction, from the annals of early America. The course of development and rules of governance will not run smoothly, but startling potential might emerge from what look to be "primitive" circumstances.

Finally, our study of this history can help us appreciate a theological truth that runs throughout the Bible. This theme has been especially emphasized in the Reformed Protestant tradition that seeded New England in Puritan form and large swatches of the Middle Colonies and the backcountry in Presbyterian guise. Under the label of "predestination" this teaching has generated no end of argument in church history, but the broader underlying historical lesson is beyond dispute. We are all of us well and truly shaped by the circumstances into which we are born, stamped by the cultures in which we are reared. Even as we try to move beyond these—maybe especially when we try to reject them—we take them along. At the same time, the "Calvinists" who affirm this doctrine have always been quick to distinguish it from fatalism. We are also endowed with a range of free choices. We can see through our inheritance and sort out its less worthy elements. We are called to attend to the divine grace that can deliver us from captivity to our origins and from the pride of merely reacting against them. One means of that grace is learning to attend to the how's and why's of other people's experience. This is part of loving our neighbor—and of duly loving ourselves. To understand all is not to approve all, but to duly appreciate what has been and aspire to what yet may be.

Further Reading

Early America is the subject of some excellent textbooks that include detailed lists of the rich and copious scholarship on every topic in the field. These titles include Gary B. Nash, *Red, White, and Black: The Peoples of Early North America*, 7th edition (Boston: Prentice Hall, 2014); Alan Taylor, *American Colonies: The Settling of North America* (New York: Penguin, 2001); Richard Middleton, *Colonial America: A History, 1585–1776* (Cambridge, Mass.: Blackwell, 1992); and T. H. Breen and Timothy Hall, *Colonial America in an Atlantic World: A Story of Creative Interaction* (New York: Pearson, 2004).

The definitive treatment of the comparative-regional approach followed in this book is David Hackett Fischer, *Albion's Seed: Four British Folkways in America* (New York and Oxford: Oxford University Press, 1989). A more popular version is Colin Woodard, *American Nations: A History of the Eleven Rival Regional Cultures of North America* (New York: Viking, 2011). More focused treatments include E. Digby Baltzell, *Puritan Boston and Quaker Philadelphia: Two Protestant Ethics and the Spirit* of Class Authority and Leadership (New York: Free Press, 1979); and T. H. Breen, Puritans and Adventurers: Change and Persistence in Early America (New York and Oxford: Oxford University Press, 1980).

The best overview of African-American life in this era is Ira Berlin, Many Thousands Gone: The First Two Centuries of Slavery in North America (Cambridge, Mass.: Harvard University Press, 1998). Philip D. Morgan, Slave Counterpoint: Black Culture in the Eighteenth-Century Chesapeake and Lowcountry (Chapel Hill: University of North Carolina Press, 1998), provides the best inter-regional comparison. Study of Native American life should begin with Daniel K. Richter, Facing East from Indian Country: A Native History of Early America (Cambridge, Mass.: Harvard University Press, 2001).

Modern scholarship on early Virginia has been defined by Edmund S. Morgan, American Slavery, American Freedom: The Ordeal of Colonial Virginia (New York: W. W. Norton, 1975). T. H. Breen, Tobacco Culture: The Mentality of the Tidewater Planters on the Eve of the Revolution (Princeton, N.J.: Princeton University Press, 1985), amplifies the culturalist approach taken in this book. Richard S. Dunn, Sugar and Slaves: The Rise of the Planter Class in the English West Indies, 1624–1713 (Chapel Hill, N.C.: University of North Carolina Press, 1998), explores the backdrop to the history of the Lower South. See also Philip D. Curtin, The Rise and Fall of the Plantation Complex: Essays in Atlantic History (New York and Cambridge:

Cambridge University Press, 1998). Robert M. Weir, *Colonial South Carolina: A History* (Columbia, S.C.: University of South Carolina Press, 1997); and Marjoleine Kars, *Breaking Loose Together: The Regulator Rebellion in Pre-Revolutionary North Carolina* (Chapel Hill, N.C.: University of North Carolina Press, 2002), detail the history of those two colonies.

Joseph Conforti, *Saints and Strangers: New England in British North America* (Baltimore: Johns Hopkins University Press, 2006), is the state-of-the-art study of that region. David D. Hall, *A Reforming People: Puritanism and the Transformation of Public Life in New England* (New York: Knopf, 2011), is the current standard on Puritan studies. The Middle Colonies' relationships among religion, ethnicity, and politics are laid out well in Gary B. Nash, *Quakers and Politics: Pennsylvania, 1681–1726* (Boston: Northeastern University Press, 1993); and Alan Tully, *Forming American Politics: Ideals, Interests, and Institutions in Colonial New York and Pennsylvania* (Baltimore: Johns Hopkins University Press, 1994). James G. Leyburn, *The Scotch-Irish: A Social History* (Chapel Hill, N.C.: University of North Carolina Press, pb reprint, 1989), remains the most scholarly study of the topic. But see also, as with all the regions considered here, the relevant section of Fischer, *Albion's Seed.*

CPSIA information can be obtained
at www.ICGtesting.com
Printed in the USA
LVOW07s1258191017
553016LV00004B/556/P